EVERYDAY JOBS

BIG IDEAS: HIGH BEGINNER

KAREN RICHARDSON

WAYZGOOSE PRESS

Edited by Robyn Brinks Lockwood

Print ISBN: 978-1-961953-23-9

CONTENTS

Introduction v

Note for Teachers vii

1. Dan the Parcel Delivery Man 1
2. Sara the Clothes Shop Assistant 4
3. Anita the Airport Security Officer 7
4. Martha the Care Worker 10
5. Omar the Taxi Driver 13
6. Mina the Gardener 16
7. Petra the Traffic Warden 19
8. Bryan the Odd-Job Man 22
9. Leon the Library Assistant 25
10. Daisy the Restaurant Server 28
11. Max the Dog Walker 31
12. Valerie the Volunteer 34

INTRODUCTION

Dear *Everyday Jobs* readers,

We hope you enjoy the twelve short stories in this book. You can use the stories in many different ways. You can read silently, or out loud to a friend. You can read into a voice recorder and then listen to your pronunciation. In this book, you will read about people and the jobs they do. You can read the stories in any order.

Many common English words are in the stories. This book will help you practice reading and speaking English. You will read short words, but also longer words and sentences.

Everyday Jobs has stories with words for everyday work situations. All the stories contain dialogue and so you can practice conversations with the stories. The stories are easy to understand and include some special words and phrases for each job. You and your family might do similar jobs to the people in this book. The stories will help you read fluently, and the questions at the end of each story will help you talk about your job.

At the end of the book you can write about your job, and there are questions you can ask a friend about their job.

We hope you enjoy reading *Everyday Jobs*.

Karen Richardson, author and teacher

NOTE FOR TEACHERS

All the chapters in this book are based on interviews with people who actually do these jobs. Names and location details have been changed, but the rest of the information comes directly from real work-life situations. (Note: this book is written in British English.)

Each short chapter is followed by two questions which encourage learners to use some of the language they have just read and to talk about their own experiences.

The book can be read by students outside of class with the help of a dictionary, or in class with your support. The book is written at high A1/ low A2 level. Around 75-80% of the words are A1, the majority of the rest are A2. However, there are some words that we need in order to talk about specific jobs and work in general that are above this level, for example, shifts, volunteer and delivery. Some of the higher level words are cognates and so the students will know similar words in their own language and therefore be able to understand them. Because other job-specific words will be useful for students, we have decided to keep them in the chapters when no equivalent lower-level words are available. Where possible, these are included in the illustrations.

Each chapter contains examples of things that people typically say in each job, or things they are often asked. These small sections of dialogue will help give students the confidence to communicate with people at work and in everyday situations. Why not encourage students to use them in role plays of their own creation?

At the end of the book there is a questionnaire for students to fill out about their own work. They can use words they have learnt from the stories to do this. After they have completed it for themselves, they can use the second questionnaire in a communicative group task in which students interview each other about their jobs and write down the answers.

1

DAN THE PARCEL DELIVERY MAN

Dan is carrying some parcels.

Dan is a university student. In the holidays, he works full-time as a parcel delivery man.

"Good morning. I have a parcel for you," says Dan.

"Just a moment. I'm coming down," says the woman in apartment 5A.

"Please sign here," says Dan. "And can you take this parcel for your neighbour in 5B?"

"Of course," says Dan's customer.

"Thanks," says Dan. "And have a nice day!"

Dan is a friendly young man and he's always on time. That's important in his job. Dan drives a company van. He needs a driving licence, and he must be a good driver. He must also be fit and strong because some parcels are heavy.

Dan starts work early in the morning. He works six days a week. First, he puts the parcels into his van. Then he drives around the town and takes the parcels to his customers.

Delivery people wear uniforms in their company colours. In summer, Dan wears shorts and a cap. In winter, he wears long trousers, a big jacket, and a hat that keeps his head and his ears warm.

Dan doesn't earn much money. He gets 13 euros an hour. He is very happy when his customers give him a tip.

Some people order a lot of things from online shops. They get parcels every day. They are always happy to see Dan.

Reflection

1. What things do you buy online? How many parcels did you get last month?
2. Who delivers them to you? Do you tip your delivery person?

2

SARA THE CLOTHES SHOP ASSISTANT

A customer is paying Sara with her credit card.

"Can I help you?" Sara asks the customer.

"I'd like to try these on," the customer says. "Where are the changing rooms?"

"At the back of the shop. Call me if you need any help," Sara says.

"Do you have this dress in a different colour?" asks the customer, looking at herself in the mirror.

"Yes, in yellow and green," answers Sara. "Is the size okay?"

"Hmm. It's a bit big. I'd like to try the dress in yellow in a smaller size," says the customer.

Sara goes to the clothes rail to look for the dress.

"Oh, I'm sorry, we only have it in green in the smaller size. Try it on, and if it fits, I can order the yellow dress in that size," Sara says. "I'll be back in a moment." She goes to help another customer who wants to buy a gift voucher.

Some days the clothes shop is quiet, but on other days, like today, everybody wants Sara's help at the same time. Her colleague is sick today, so she's on her own in the shop. Sara is happy that it is Saturday and that the shop is not open tomorrow.

The first customer takes the green dress to the cash desk where Sara is talking to a man who wants to return a pair of jeans.

"I'm going to buy the green dress," says the first customer.

Sara takes the dress and scans the price tag.

"That's £89,99," she says. "How would you like to pay?"

"By card," says the customer.

"Tap your card here, please," Sara says and gives the customer the card machine. "Great, thanks. And here's your receipt," Sara says. "Do you need a bag?"

"Yes, please," the customer says.

Sara puts the green dress and the receipt into the bag and gives it to the customer.

"Thanks for your help," the customer says.

"You're welcome," Sara says. "Now, who's next?" she says to the four people waiting for her help.

Reflection

1. What is your favourite clothes shop? Where is it? Why do you like it?
2. Where do you buy clothes? Do you pay for new clothes with a card, with cash, or some other way?

3

ANITA THE AIRPORT SECURITY OFFICER

Anita is searching a passenger at the airport.

Anita says, "Next!" and "This way please" hundreds of times an hour. Anita is an airport security officer at Heathrow Airport in London. She works in a team of four people. They check thousands of passengers and their bags every day.

"Put your keys and phone here," Anita says. "Is this your bag?"

The bags go through an x-ray machine. Anita and her colleagues can see what is inside the bags.

Passengers must stand in a body scanner. When the alarm sounds, Anita says, "May I search you please, madam?" or, "Please take off your shoes and belt, sir."

She holds a metal detector in her hand to check for knives and other sharp and dangerous items.

The airport is open twenty-four hours a day. Anita and her team do shift work. There are three shifts: the morning shift, the afternoon and evening shift, and the night shift. They wear a uniform at work. They always wear gloves when they search passengers and their bags.

Anita has many stories about the strange things people have in their luggage. One woman had her pet rat in her handbag. A man had a rucksack full of cash. One time, Anita found a gun in a man's bag. He said it was his son's toy gun, but it wasn't a toy. Anita and her colleagues help to keep passengers and airline staff safe.

Reflection

1. Anita works at Heathrow Airport. Is it a large or a small airport? Have you flown

through Heathrow or another airport in England?

2. Where is your nearest airport? Is it large or small? Where can you fly to from this airport?

4

MARTHA THE CARE WORKER

Martha talks to Mrs Miller.

Martha opens the curtains and says, "Good morning, Mrs Miller. How are you today? Did you sleep well?"

"Good morning..." Mrs Miller can't remember Martha's name.

"Martha," says Martha.

"Can you help me get up, Martha?" Mrs Miller asks.

Martha raises the back of the electric bed so that Mrs Miller can sit up.

"It's a lovely day, Mrs Miller. I'll open the window. Would you like a cup of tea?" she asks.

"Oh yes, please. With milk and sugar. Can you help me to the bathroom first?" Mrs Miller asks.

"Of course," Martha says. She helps Mrs Miller to get out of bed. They walk slowly to the bathroom together. Luckily for Martha, Mrs Miller is a small woman. Some of the people who live in the care home are big and heavy. It's hard work and Martha's back hurts all the time.

"I'll wait outside the bathroom. Don't lock the door. And call me if you need my help," Martha tells Mrs Miller.

Soon, Mrs Miller is back in her room. Martha helps her sit down at the table and goes to get the breakfast. She comes back with Mrs Miller's breakfast: toast and butter, a soft egg, and a nice hot cup of tea with milk and sugar.

"Thank you. You're a good girl, Martha," Mrs Miller says.

Martha is young, but she doesn't feel like a girl. Sometimes she feels as old as Mrs Miller.

"I'm happy to help you. It's my job," Martha says. "I'm going next door to Mr Smith now. Before I go, is there anything else you need?"

"A cup of tea would be lovely," Mrs Miller says.

"You have a cup of tea. It's on the table in front of you," Martha says.

"Oh, do I? Oh yes, there it is. Oh, there's milk in my tea. I don't like milk," Mrs Miller says.

"I'll bring you another cup of tea," Martha says. "I'll be back in a moment."

Mrs Miller looks out of the window. She hopes her mother will take her to the park today.

Reflection

1. Do you know anyone who lives or works in a care home? What do they like about working or living there?
2. Think about the older people you know. Where do they live? Where do you want to live when you are old?

5

OMAR THE TAXI DRIVER

"Where do you want to go?" asks Omar.

Omar gets out of the car and rings the doorbell. "Your taxi is here," he says.

"Great, I'll be there in a moment," the customer says.

"Can I help you with your suitcase?" Omar asks.

He puts the suitcase into the taxi and waits for his customer. Omar likes driving. He especially likes driving customers to the airport. He likes to hear about their holidays and business trips. Airport customers are usually happy. Some are flying to see their family in another country.

Omar thinks of his family. He hopes they can join him soon. He drives the taxi every day. He never takes a day off. He needs to earn money so that his wife and children can come to live with him in this new country.

Back home, he had his own business. He didn't have a boss. Here, he has a boss who tells him what to do and where to go. Omar drives people to the airport, to the station, and to the hospital. He talks to the customers and that helps him improve his English. Sometimes it is difficult to understand what they say, especially the Saturday night customers.

On Saturdays around midnight, Omar waits with other taxis in the town centre. The Saturday night customers come from clubs and discos and sometimes they have had a lot to drink. He looks after them and drives them home.

He likes to talk with the other taxi drivers. Like Omar, many of them had a very different life in their home country. Alexi was a doctor. Yuri was a teacher. And Dana was a police officer.

"Here we are. Terminal Two," Omar says and parks the taxi.

"Thank you," the customer says as she pays the taxi fare. "And this is for you," she says, giving Omar a big tip.

"Thank you very much," he says. "Have a good flight."

Reflection

1. Do you have a car? Do you like driving? What do you like and not like about driving?
2. Would you like to be a taxi driver? Why or why not?

6

MINA THE GARDENER

Mina loves working with plants.

It's 7.30 in the morning. Mina parks her company van in front of her client's house. It's going to be very hot and sunny this afternoon so Mina must start work early today. She rings the doorbell. Ding dong.

"Good morning," she says. Her client, Mrs Bishop, opens the garden gate.

"Come around the house into the garden," Mrs. Bishop tells her.

Mina gets her tools from the back of the van and takes them into the garden. She wears green work trousers and a green t-shirt with her company name. Mina is self-employed. She has her own gardening business.

Sometimes she wears big heavy boots, but today she doesn't need them. She did the hard garden work yesterday. Yesterday, she and her apprentice put down a path, cut the trees, put up three bird houses, and made a small pond. It was a long day. Today, her apprentice is at college and Mina is working alone.

"I've got the plants and wildflower seeds you ordered, and I have some other plants for the pond," Mina says. "First, I'll put in the flowers and water plants, and then I'll start the wildflower garden. Soon you'll have butterflies, bees, and other insects. And maybe a frog in the pond."

Mrs Bishop claps her hands. "I'm so happy with my new garden," she says. "Birds came to the pond yesterday evening. One had a bath in the water."

Mina puts on her hat, pulls on her gloves, and starts work.

"I'll plant these first and water them well. It's going to be hot this afternoon," she says.

"Would you like a cup of coffee?" Mrs Bishop asks.

"Not yet, thanks. I should do some work first," Mina says.

"I'll bring you a coffee in about an hour, then. Black, no sugar, like yesterday. And I'll bring you a slice of cake, too," Mrs Bishop says.

"Lovely," Mina says.

Reflection

1. Do you have a garden or a balcony? Do you have any house plants? Which is your favourite?
2. What do you like in a garden? Describe your dream garden.

7

PETRA THE TRAFFIC WARDEN

Petra checks the man's license.

Petra works outside. She does a lot of walking, and she needs good shoes. She has a uniform with a cap to keep off the rain. She works in all kinds of weather, and she works on weekends and holidays. She usually works alone. Today, she is in the city centre.

Petra stops walking and stands next to a car. A man in a shop sees her and runs to the car.

"Is this your car?" she asks.

"Yes, it is," he answers.

"You can't park here. This is a no-parking area," she tells him.

"I'm just waiting for my sick mother. She's at the doctor," he says.

She doesn't believe him. People often tell her stories that are not true.

"You can park in the next street," she tells him. "But not here. I won't write you a ticket today, but you must move your car immediately."

The man gets in his car and drives away.

Petra must stay calm and be polite to drivers even when they are angry. She knows how to be strict. She has three teenage sons at home.

She walks around the corner and gets out her camera. She takes a photo of an expensive sports car parked in a disabled bay. The car does not have a disabled sticker. This time she writes a ticket. The driver must pay a fine. Petra's mother is in a wheelchair. She has no sympathy for people who park in disabled parking spaces.

"Excuse me. Can you help me? I don't know how to

work this ticket machine," a woman says. "Where do I put the money?"

"The new machines don't take cash. You need to download the app on your phone or pay by card," she explains. "Here, let me show you."

"Thank you. You are very kind," the woman says.

Reflection

1. Is it easy to park where you live? Where must you not park?
2. How much does it cost to park for two hours in the city centre?

8

BRYAN THE ODD-JOB MAN

Bryan paints the house wall.

"No job is too big or too small." That's what it says on the side of Bryan's van. It's not really true, but the customers like it. Bryan likes the small jobs that he can do inside a customer's house. He likes working in people's houses.

"When can you put up my new lights, Bryan?" a customer asks on the phone.

"I have time on Friday. Is that okay for you?" he asks.

"Yes, Friday is good. And can you clear out the rubbish from my garage, too?" she asks.

That's an easy job. Bryan can do that. He can do many things. He can paint walls, put a new lock on the door, replace a broken window, make new book shelves... anything really. He'll do any odd job around the house or garden. If it's a big job and he needs help, he always knows someone who can help him.

Bryan puts down his paintbrush and stands back to look at his work. Today, Bryan is painting a customer's garden shed where she keeps her garden tools, her flower pots, and her seeds. The customer is at work and he is on his own. He likes that. He is happy when he can work alone. He can listen to his radio and his podcasts and hear about what is happening in the world. He often eats his lunch in his van, but today he can eat it in the customer's garden.

Three years ago, Bryan was a stressed and unhappy businessman. He wore a suit to his office in the city and worked 12 hours a day. Then he lost his job. It was the happiest day of his life.

"You did good work on that shed," a neighbour says

from the next garden. "I need someone to put up my curtains. Can you do that for me?"

Of course he can. No job is too big or too small.

Reflection

1. What odd jobs could Bryan do at your home?
2. Which job would you prefer: doing odd jobs or being a businessperson in the city? Why?

9

LEON THE LIBRARY ASSISTANT

Leon checks the books.

The job of a library assistant is not the same as it was 20 years ago. These days, a library is more than just a large building with books.

"Do you have the *Star Wars* movies?" a young woman asks.

"Yes. The DVDs are on the second floor next to the computer work stations," Leon says.

Leon works Tuesday to Saturday. The library is not open on Monday. From Tuesday to Friday, many school pupils come to the library in their lunch break or after school to do their homework.

"Is it okay to drink this here?" a teenager asks.

"Yes, you can drink here, but please don't eat your burger in here," Leon says.

The library's Reading Café sells drinks and cakes on Saturdays. This café is a place where older men like to spend the morning. They sit at the tables, drink coffee, and read magazines and newspapers while their wives go shopping in the town.

Leon puts books and DVDs back in the right shelves and helps people find what they need. But there is a lot more to his job. He also looks after the library's social media. Every day, he posts a book tip or information about the library.

The library often has special events and story afternoons for children, and sometimes there is a talk or music in the evening for adults.

"What time is the puppet theatre next week?" a mother asks.

"It's at three o'clock on Thursday afternoon," Leon answers. "There aren't many tickets left."

"Okay, I'd like three tickets, please," the mother says.

Leon gives her the tickets.

In his job, he needs to know a lot about computers, social media, books, comics, audiobooks, video and computer games, and DVDs.

"The paper is stuck again," a boy calls.

Leon must also know how to work the photocopier.

His job is never boring.

Reflection

1. Is there a library where you live? What do they have there?
2. What was the last book you read? What was it about? Did you like it?

10

DAISY THE RESTAURANT SERVER

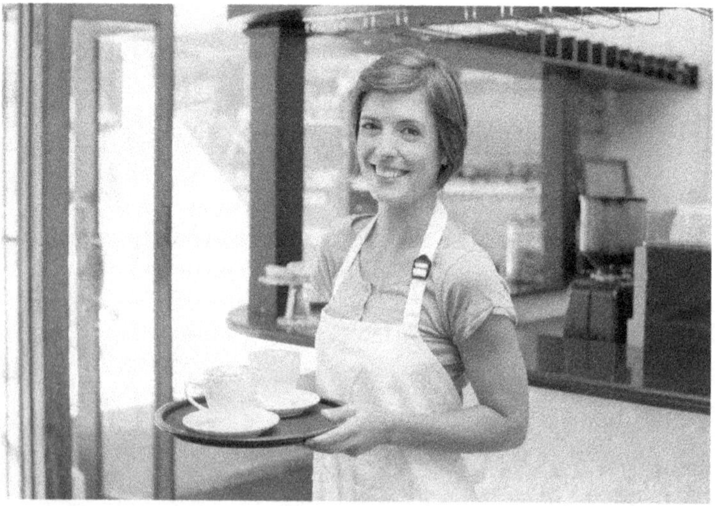

Daisy is serving coffee.

The customer looks at Daisy and closes his menu. She walks to his table.

"Are you ready to order?" she asks.

"Yes, I'd like the roast chicken, please," he answers.

"Would you like fries or salad with the chicken?" Daisy asks.

"Hmm, the fries sound good. But, no, I'll have the salad today. Or maybe I'll have the fries... No, salad is better for me, but I like fries... hmm..."

Daisy stands and waits for the customer to decide. She works as a server in a restaurant. She doesn't get much money in her job, but she always tries to be helpful. When she is friendly and polite to the customers, they often give her a good tip.

"Why don't I bring you chicken and fries and a side salad?" she says to the customer.

"That sounds good," the customer says. "And can I have another glass of water, too?"

"Of course. I'll bring that now," Daisy says. Daisy goes to the kitchen to give the meal order to the cook. Then she walks to the bar, gets the drink, and takes it to the customer. Daisy walks and stands for many hours at work. When she gets home, her feet hurt.

"Excuse me. We'd like to pay. Can we have the bill, please?" asks a customer at another table.

"Certainly," says Daisy. She takes away the plates and empty water bottle and brings the customer his bill.

"Did you enjoy your meal?" she asks.

"Yes, it was very nice. And the service was excellent. This is for you," the customer says as he gives her a big tip. Daisy is happy. For a moment, she forgets that her feet hurt and that it's Saturday and she must work until midnight.

Reflection

1. When did you last go to a restaurant? What did you eat and drink? Did the server do a good job?
2. Your restaurant bill is 56 euros. The service was very good and you enjoyed the meal. How much do you give the server as a tip?

11

MAX THE DOG WALKER

Max is walking a lot of dogs!

There were always a lot of animals in Max's life. When he was a child, he lived in the countryside. He grew up on a farm with cows, sheep, goats, ducks, chickens, and lots of dogs and cats. When he came to this country, he had to move into a small apartment on the second floor. Everything else was too expensive. He doesn't have a garden or a balcony, and he cannot have a pet.

He didn't have a job at first, and he was sad and bored. He often sat in the park opposite his apartment with his lunch and his English books. Two years ago, he met a man and a dog in the park. The man looked worried.

"My poor dog," the man said. "My boss says I can't work from home anymore. I must go back to the office, every day, Monday to Friday."

"I can walk your dog for you," Max said. "I love animals." And that was the beginning of his job as a dog walker.

Now, Max walks dogs for seven different clients. He walks four small dogs together in the morning. They play and run together, and they are always very funny. Then he walks one difficult dog at lunchtime. And in the afternoon, he walks two bigger dogs.

He does a lot of walking, and so he doesn't need to go to the gym. He and the dogs get a lot of exercise. He also meets a lot of people. People don't talk to you when you are on your own, but they often stop and talk to you when you walk dogs.

It's midday and Max arrives at his client's house. He

opens the door and the dog runs to say hello. Max's four-legged clients are always very happy to see him.

"Who's a good boy?" he says to Marley. "Are you ready for your walk?"

Max has keys to all his clients' houses. He takes their dogs out while they are at work.

"Come on, boy," he says to Marley. "Let's go to the park. Where's your ball?"

Reflection

1. Do you like dogs? Do you think you would like being a dog walker? Why or why not?
2. Did you have any pets when you were a child? What were they? What did you name them?

12

VALERIE THE VOLUNTEER

Valerie helps a child practice reading.

It's 9.00 in the morning and Valerie is at school. She's in the second-grade classroom with the eight-year-old children. There are twenty-five pupils in the class. There are children of eleven different nationalities, and they speak thirteen languages.

Valerie volunteers one morning a week at the school to help the class teacher. She doesn't get any money for helping in the class. She is a volunteer. Valerie is 48 years old and her own three children are now adults. She loves children and wants to help her community.

"What did you do at the weekend?" she asks the children at her table. The children all want to tell her about their weekend. She helps them find words and to speak in long sentences. Storytelling is a good way for the children to learn to speak English well.

"Where does your grandmother live?" she asks a girl who is very quiet and doesn't talk much. Many children like to tell stories about their families in other countries.

It's time for the first lesson. Valerie walks around the classroom and helps children to organise themselves.

"Write your name on the worksheet," she says. "Where's your pen? Is it in your school bag? Where's your school bag?"

"Can you help me, please?" one child asks.

"Of course," Valerie says. She likes it when children say *please* and *thank you*.

A big part of her job is to show the children that they are clever and that they *can* do things. She helps them one time, and next time they can do it by themselves.

"That's very good," she says. "Well done."

Valerie wears clothes and jewellery in bright, friendly colours. It helps her connect with the children. Today, she is wearing a red shirt.

"Look, I have a red shirt, too!" one girl says.

"And my dress is red. Let's take a selfie," another girl says.

Valerie takes out her phone and takes a photo. The children all crowd around her to look at the photo on the screen.

"Okay, now it's time to practise reading," she says. "Please get out your reading books."

Reflection

1. Where did you go to school? Who was your favourite teacher? Were there any volunteers that helped your class?
2. What kind of volunteer work do you do/would you like to do?

www.ingramcontent.com/pod-product-compliance
Lightning Source LLC
Chambersburg PA
CBHW021119020426
42331CB00004B/552
9781961953239